"SPEECH CRAFTERS"
PUBLIC SPEAKING FOR CHILDREN AND YOUNG ADULTS

Copyright © 2014 by Beverly Jones-Durr
Published by: Gifted Genie Publishing
Madison, AL 35757
ISBN 978-0-9897187-2-1
All Rights Reserved
Printed in the United States of America

Contents

Course Overview ------------------------------- 4
Lesson One ------------------------------- 5
Lesson Two ------------------------------- 7
Lesson Three ------------------------------- 15
Lesson Four ------------------------------- 18
Lesson Five ------------------------------- 21
Lesson Six ------------------------------- 25
Lesson Seven ------------------------------- 29

Forms

Evaluation – All About You ---------------- 31
Evaluation – Organizing your Speech ---- 32
Practice Exercise ---------------------------- 33
Evaluation - Gestures ---------------------- 34
Evaluation – Voice, Vocab, Variation ---- 36
Evaluation - Persuasive ------------------ 38
Evaluation – Entertain ------------------ 40
Ashton's Public Speaking Tips --------- 42
Aidyn's Speaking Pointers ------------- 43

This course is intended to help you as a new speaker gain confidence by writing and presenting a variety of speeches. These speeches will be thoroughly researched and filled with your personal creativity. How is that done? Glad you asked. Let me first explain the history of public speaking. For years people have been speaking to groups of people instructing them on a lot of subjects. By taking an active part in this course, you will have the opportunity to develop skills and gain the self-confidence needed to be a good speaker. Students are presented the basic elements of a speech, the introduction, the body and the conclusion. Students will learn how to use their voices with clarity. The use of body gestures, facial expressions as well as eye contact requires careful instruction. You will have at your disposal speaking tips, preparation assistance, guidance in constructing the proper speech and various speaking objectives meant to increase your speaking skills and fine tune your poise all while having fun. Each speech will be evaluated providing feedback on presentation, delivery and construction. Improvement suggestions will also be offered as well as acknowledgement of skills learned and performed.

Lesson One

All About You

Introducing a speaker is an important part of the speaking process. A proper introduction provides pertinent information to the audience. The speaker is identified by name along with the title of the speech. The objectives of the speech are also included so that the audience has an idea of what to expect. The person introducing the speaker is called the Leader or Announcer. You might be asked to perform this function. Instruction on the proper performance of this duty will be discussed later.

For your first speech, you are asked to tell the audience <u>All About You</u>. You may speak about hobbies, friends, trips you've taken, favorite flowers, best subjects in school, etc. The point to this speech is:

1. Help the audience to get to know who you are and what your likes and/or dislikes are.

2. *This is the initial evaluation of your current speaking skills. Revealing your strengths and weaknesses will enable the course to be in tune with your public speaking skills.*
3. *This speech is timed. You must speak at least 3 minutes but no more than 5 minutes.*

Here's a cheat sheet to get you started:

1. *Name*
2. *Brothers, Sisters – interesting facts about them*
3. *Hobbies or interests*
4. *Favorite subject in school and why*
5. *What is it that people like about you?*
6. *The one thing most people do not know about you.*
7. *Who is your best friend and why?*

Evaluation form for this speech can be found on page 31. This is a self-evaluation. You will also be evaluated by the instructor to determine your current level of speaking skills.

Lesson Two

Introduction to Public Speaking

Now that you have completed your first speech and received feedback you are now ready to move forward towards understanding what a speech is all about. You will learn much more by doing than by simply studying in this class. Just as you can't learn to play an instrument by reading books or listening to lectures, you will not become a good speaker without getting up before an audience and speaking.

Objectives of this lesson are:

1. To learn the elements of a good speech.
2. To become familiar with the purpose and principles of evaluations.

Learning to express your thoughts and interests with clarity and logic to others helps to persuade them to your point of view. It can be really nerve wrecking thinking about standing before an audience and conveying your thoughts. Trust me, the discomfort increases when you are actually standing in front of the audience. Your palms become sweaty, your knees tremble, your mouth gets dry and your mind goes blank! I've been there, and so has every other public speaker. These are all normal reactions. Here's the good news...this too shall become manageable.

Developing Self-Confidence

Your fear of speaking in front of an audience will subside by increasing your knowledge of the subject. Pick a subject that you are knowledgeable about, one that excites you. Discussing subjects such as these will actually create enjoyment for you. In order to build self-confidence though, you have to identify what you are afraid of. Common fears include:

a. Fear of the audience
b. Fear of making a fool out of yourself

c. Fear of being boring
d. Fear that the audience will ridicule you
e. Fear that what you have to say just isn't important.

Only practice can overcome these fears. Practice! Practice! Practice!

Preparing Your Speech

Although the initial speech was all about you, it probably wasn't as easy as you thought. We just aren't real good at talking about ourselves. You could have spoken about any aspect of your identity. The first step was creating that first sentence. The first sentence is the one that grabs the audience's attention. If the sentences that follow are written correctly, you will hold their attention right up to the conclusion. So let's break it down into three equally important parts.

The Introduction: This part of the speech starts with your opening sentence. For instance, if your speech is to inform and persuade you might start out by indicating that something is wrong. Continue by stating what is wrong, who is to blame and what harm has occurred as a result.

The Body: Using the example above, you might want to indicate whether this wrong can be corrected and make several recommendations as to how the correction might be done.

The Conclusion: Tell the audience what you want them to do or how they are to react. This is your opportunity to be excited, passionate and sincere and end with a call to action.

All great speeches must include these three elements in order to be deemed successful. Without them, your audience will miss your point and you will have missed an opportunity to be effective.

Practice Time

You have got to make time to practice your speech. It is okay to have notes, but it is not okay to read your speech to the audience. They are looking forward to hearing and seeing you present your speech. This is what sets you apart from the audience. If they wanted to hear you read to them...well they could have done that for themselves. Remember, the more you practice the less nervous and fearful you'll be. Partner up with a friend or practice in front of a mirror. Seeing yourself as you deliver your speech during practice can be very enlightening. Remember, try to relax and have fun. After all who knows more about you than YOU? Don't forget to smile. A smile always puts your audience at ease and creates calm in you.

Speaking: There are a few things all speakers do once introduced. Once you have been introduced approach the front of the audience. It should already be clear where each speaker will stand to present their speech. Once there, acknowledge the person who introduced you with a hand shake and proceed to face the audience. You should begin your speech with "Ladies and Gentlemen", pause briefly and then say your opening sentence. Don't fidget with your clothes or sway from side to side. Use your hands to make simple gestures and you may take a few steps left and right while maintaining eye contact with the audience. A good trick is to look left and then right and then towards the back of the room and in front pausing for a few seconds on each direction. Speak loud enough that the audience in the back of the room can hear you. Don't rush your words. Speak clearly. Your speech will be timed so pay close attention to the timer who is generally sitting in front. When ending, please do not say "Thank you", just close with your prepared ending sentence and turn towards the introducer. This is an indication that your speech is finished. Wait for the applause and then leave the speaking area.

Evaluations

The important part of self-improvement is feedback. Feedback allows us to learn how well we did and where we need improvement. Every speech you write and present will be evaluated. The evaluation form will be completed by the audience (class).

Roles: A speech presentation can include several key roles besides the speaker. They include:
1. Announcer: responsible for introducing the speaker to the audience. Also serves as the leader of the speech making sessions.
2. Timer: All speeches are timed. The role of timer is to keep track of how long a speaker presents and to keep the speaker on target. The color system is used. Green indicates the speaker has spoken for 3 minutes, Yellow indicates 4 minutes and Red indicates 5 minutes. After the red card is shown the speaker will have 30 seconds to close.

3. *Grammarian:* grammar and vocabulary is important to the speech process. The grammarian makes note of grammar usage good or bad. The grammarian also maintains a list of words with definition so speakers might expand their vocabulary.
4. *Evaluator:* It's important to understand that the evaluator isn't a judge nor your enemy. The evaluator will be offering feedback to strengthen your speaking skills. Don't become defensive. The evaluation is essential to help improve the quality of your speech writing and speaking skills. One is assigned for each speaker.

Speech Time

Evaluation form is on page 32. Here are your objectives:

<u>Organize Your Speech:</u> You are to develop a speech using the key elements of introduction, body and conclusion. You may choose any topic for your speech. Use the guidelines of lesson two to help you prepare. This speech will be timed. You must speak at least three (3) minutes and no more than five (5) minutes. Speakers meeting the timing requirement will have a chance to receive a ribbon for best speaker of the day. The evaluator is also eligible to receive a ribbon for best evaluator of the day. Voting will be completed by audience (class). Ballots will be provided. Speeches must be written and submitted to the instructor the day before your scheduled speech is presented to the audience. Your speech will be reviewed and your will receive an instructor evaluation after presenting your speech to the audience. Your instructor will provide the method you will use to submit your speech during class time.

Lesson Three

Equally as important as being a great speaker is learning to become a great listener. Just because you aren't talking when someone is presenting a speech doesn't mean you are listening. You could be thinking about your plans for lunch or dinner, whether or not you passed that pop quiz earlier today, even what your plans are for the weekend. If you aren't listening how will you learn anything? If you aren't listening you might miss the speaker's point of view. Listening is an important skill that often goes neglected. Here are a few bad habits most people have when it comes to listening:

1. *Criticizing the speaker's appearance.*
2. *Getting overly excited or even angry about something the speaker says.*
3. *Taking too many notes. Sometimes you miss important factors while writing.*

4. Pretending to be paying attention to the speaker. This one can really leave you with egg on your face if the speaker happens to ask you a question. Embarrassing!
5. Creating or even tolerating distractions...cell phones, audience chatter, etc.
6. Deciding that the subject of the speech is boring and uninteresting before the speaker utters a single word.
7. Waiting for your opportunity to interject your point and interrupting.

Here's how to be a good listener:

1. Look the speaker in the eyes.
2. Sit calmly and quietly and pay attention.
3. Limit your movement.
4. Have an expression of enjoyment on your face. Smile, laugh when appropriate, it puts the speaker at ease.
5. Ask questions when allowed.

6. Listen to the speaker to learn if he or she speaks clearly and whether the speech is organized. You should be able to summarize the speech afterwards.
7. Be willing to listen.
8. Be nonthreatening.
9. Respect the speaker's point of view.

Hearing is just one step in the listening process. Listening involves receiving, organizing, interpreting, and responding to the information that is heard. Being a good listener enables the speaker to feel good about their performance. Your encouragement of the speaker will build their confidence. Your skills as a good listener will also help you to become a better speaker and will play a vital role in your success.

Practice Exercise: Let's see how well you use the information above to improve your listening skills. Turn to page 32 and complete the exercise based upon what you *heard* during lesson four. Were you listening?

Lesson Four

Gestures When Speaking

Objectives of this lesson:

1. Discover the importance of gestures in speaking.
2. Understanding when and how to use them.

Gestures are an important and powerful body language. They emphasize points, relax an audience, and help the audience understand important parts of your speech. Often, gestures are the only visual expression your audience will get. You are showing them what you mean as well as telling them.

Gestures show:

1. Weight
2. Size
3. Shape
4. Direction
5. Location
6. Importance

7. Urgency.
8. Comparison
9. Contrast
10. Humor
11. Sadness

Gestures should be big enough to be seen by the whole audience. But, don't exaggerate your gestures because it will distract attention from the speech. A gesture is considered a good gesture if it helps the audience to understand the message of the speech. Be fluid. Move around calmly but purposefully. Your speaking area should not exceed a few inches beyond your podium. Remember, when introduced it has already been decided where the speakers will stand. Make a mental note of your total speaking area. That is your speech maneuvering area. Stick to it!

Speech Time

You are to prepare a speech using all the information you have learned about gestures. Make sure you are comfortable with the topic and that you have chosen one that will allow for excellent display of gestures. This speech will be timed. It should be at least three (3) minutes but no more than five (5) minutes long. The evaluation form can be found on page 34. Have Fun!

Lesson Five

Voice, Vocabulary, Variations

Have you sat through a speech that was overloaded with "big words?" Vocabulary is important, but if your speech uses words that your audience doesn't understand...what's the point? If your speech is about backyard gardening would it make any sense to use words like horticulturists, hydroponics or agronomical? Well, I suppose if you were a professor lecturing an agricultural class...but chances are you are not. Don't throw around "big words" just to impress your audience. They won't be impress...they'll be disconnected and you will lose their attention.

Instead, consider your audience...who they are, what their interests are and what you want them to take away from your speech. It is more important to be understood than to impress.

Your voice is something you normally don't pay much attention to...but we should. All people have different tones and some of those tones can be good to listen to and then...there are other tones that drive you nuts! Monotones are those where the speaker speaks on a flat line. It's almost robotic. Don't do that! Instead practice your tone. Have a friend listen to you when you are talking. Ask them to listen to see if your voice is easy to hear and understand. Do you pronounce your words fully or use slang? Is your tone high pitched? Practice in the mirror. I know I've mentioned practicing in the mirror before. It's because it's important for you to see and hear what your audience will see and hear.

Your voice is the best tool in your delivery toolbox. If you can learn to really use it well, it can distinguish one speaker from another. Variations include four things...pace, pitch, power and pauses.

1. Pace: One way to use this variation is to learn to slow down through key statements.

2. *Pitch:* This variation requires emotional content and presentation. A sad voice emphasizes a sad situation. An excited voice demonstrates happiness. Use your feelings to help convey your message to the audience.
3. *Power:* Combine your variations in volume and emotional content. Anger or joy tends to be a louder voice, whereas sadness and fear calls for the use of a quieter voice.
4. *Pauses:* Your speech has many places to use pauses in a beneficial way. Pauses should be short at the end of sentences. Longer pauses should be saved for the end of paragraphs or at transition points within your speech.

Speech Time

(Voice, Vocabulary, Variation) You are to prepare a speech using your voice, vocabulary and variation. You may choose any topic you want, just make sure that it is a topic you feel strongly about. Remember, emotional content helps you to freely use variation in all its four forms. This speech will also be timed. It should be at least three (3) minutes but not more than five (5) minutes long. Evaluation form for this speech is on page 36. Need I say it? Have Fun!

Lesson Six

Speak to Persuade

Some of the most memorable speeches can be heard in advertisements. They are short and sweet but they are persuasive. Who doesn't want to new iPad after seeing and hearing those awesome Apple commercials on TV? Persuasive speeches do three things:

Inspire — You excite the audience about your topic using your words and everything you've learned so far in this course. Sermons and commencement addresses are persuasive speeches.

Convince — Your speech should successfully change the audiences opinion to the opinion you want them to have.

Call to action — You want the audience to do something after hearing your speech...sign a petition, read a book, vote or buy a product.

In order to truly inspire your audience you have to make certain that your facts are impeccable. This requires solid research. You have to know the topic very well. You have to be sincere and your delivery must be on target. That means you have to practice!

Understand, this is not just any speech. Your audience might be agreeable, hostile, apathetic or even uninformed. Provide evidence to support your topic points. Just because you believe it to be a great idea doesn't mean everyone will. Organize your speech to make it easy to follow.

a. Present the problem/solution.
b. Make your proposal of proof
c. Compare the advantages
d. Motivate to action

Grab the audience's attention with your opening sentence. Let them know what is needed. Present your solution and explain the benefits. With your words, draw the audience a picture of how things will look after implementing your solution. Lastly, you want to make it clear what their action should be. Although this might appear to be a difficult speech...it really isn't anything you haven't seen before on your television set during an infomercial. Be creative.

Speech Time

(Persuasive) You must prepare and present a persuasive speech. As always, you will choose your topic. Follow the guidelines of this lesson. This speech will be timed. Your speech must be at least three (3) minutes but no more than five (5) minutes long. The evaluation form for this speech can be found on page 38. Have fun!

Lesson Seven

Speak to Entertain

Entertainment is an essential need of human beings. Speakers who entertain the audience include professional comedians, motivational speakers, etc. Some speeches can contain humor but they don't have to be funny to entertain. Television programs have dramas that aren't funny. They can often be quite serious, yet they are entertaining. Your approach to this type of speech depends solely on you. However, you must understand that the audience isn't looking for deep knowledge. You just want to provide them an interesting diversion.

When determining what topic to choose, think about your hobbies. You could even choose a topic that the audience might find interesting. For instance, if you are speaking to the garden club you might want to talk about an interesting time in your life or someone you know who grew the biggest pumpkin you've ever seen.

Speech Time

(Entertain) Do not forget how important of speech organizing. This is an entertaining speech. You must choose your topic. It will be timed. The speech should be at least three (3) minutes but no more than five (5) minutes long. The evaluation form for this speech can be found on page 40. Have Fun!

What Kind of Speaker am I?
(Introduction Speech)

Date:_____

The following questions are meant to help you evaluate your speaking abilities.

Do you...	yes	no
Feel comfortable talking to others?	___	___
Have trouble sharing your views or ideas?	___	___
Have nervous habits when you speak?	___	___
Practice good grammar?	___	___
Have a good vocabulary?	___	___
Listen to others and think carefully about what they are saying?	___	___
Want to improve your speaking skills?	___	___

Evaluation – Organizing Your Speech

Date: _____   Speech Title: _____

Evaluator: _____

Note: the purpose of this speech is to develop a complete speech containing an obvious open, body and closing. Speaker may choose any topic.

What was the opening of the speech?

Describe the body of the speech.

Did the speaker appear confident or nervous?

Was the speech interesting and well presented?

Describe the speech closing.

Practice Exercise

List five ways to become a good listener.

Give three examples of a bad listening habit.

Listening involves _____, _____, _____ and _____.

How does becoming a good listener help the speaker?

Evaluation of Gestures

Date:_____   Speech Title:_____

Evaluator: _____

Note: the speaker is to concentrate on organizing the speech and use gestures. There should be an open, body and conclusion. The speaker must use a variety of facial expressions, body movements and other gestures to emphasize the point of the speech.

How well did the speaker understand the goal of this speech?

Was the speech organized?

Were the speaker's gestures effective? Give examples.

Were any gestures distracting from the speakers speech?

Please offer any suggestions you feel might improve the presentation of the speech.

Evaluation – Voice Variation and Vocabulary

Date: _____   Speech Title:_____

Evaluator:_____

Note: the purpose of this speech is to use vocal variations and vocabulary within the speech to make a connection with the audience. Speaker must speak clearly with good pitch, tone and volume.

Did the speaker use vocal variations to enhance the speech?

Did the speaker talk too slowly or too fast?

Was the speaker's voice pleasant and easy to listen to?

Were the speaker's words appropriate to the audience?

Were the speaker's sentences short, simple and to the point?

Was the speaker able to create images through the use of words?

How could the speaker improve the speech?

Evaluation- Persuasive Speech

Date: _____   Speech Title:_____

Evaluator: _____

Note: The speaker must present a persuasive speech that supports his/her viewpoint on a subject they choose. This topic should be one the speaker is clearly familiar with. Speaker should be able to use less notes for this presentation.

Did the speaker project sincerity and conviction?

Was the speaker familiar with the topic?

Was the audience captured and attentive?

Did the speaker use emotion to support their viewpoint?

Was the speaker's body language and gestures helpful?

Was the speech properly organized?

Were you persuaded to accept the speaker's views?

How might the speaker improve the presentation?

Evaluation- Entertain the Audience

Date: _____   Speech Title:_____

Evaluator: _____

Note: The speaker must entertain the audience using a personal story or experience. The audience should show signs of enjoyment. Emotions and gestures should be apparent to enhancing the entertaining speech.

Could you tell that the audience was entertained? How?

How was the speech organized as you could tell?

Did the speaker use vivid descriptions and humor to entertain?

What was the speaker's strongest asset in making this speech?

How could the speaker improve the speech?

Ashton's Public Speaking Tips

Speak clear and loud enough to be heard in the back of the room.

Stand up straight.   Don't talk too fast or too slowly.

Try not to move around too much.   Use gestures and voice variation.

Don't forget to make eye contact.   Don't hide behind your notes.

Facial expressions are great! Use them.   Smile, it relaxes you.

Have fun!   If you make a mistake...keep going.

Aidyn's Speaking Pointers

Choose your words carefully.

Rehearse your speech.

Organize your speech.

Use a pleasant voice.

Don't fidget.

Write your speech so people understand.

Stay on topic.

Read your speech out loud.

Paint a picture with your words.

Use gestures when asking a question.

Show emotions when appropriate.

Notes

Notes

Notes

www.ingramcontent.com/pod-product-compliance
Lightning Source LLC
Chambersburg PA
CBHW041535040426
42446CB00002B/97